End Auto Anxiety

No Fear Car Repair And Maintenance For Busy Women

End Auto Anxiety

No Fear Car Repair And Maintenance For Busy Women

Audra Fordin

Contents

Welcome to the Least Boring Book about Cars Ever Written

Hi. My name is Audra. As a mom and auto business owner, I know what it's like to be busy. Don't worry. I won't bore you with complicated technical details. You have better things to do. Besides, you don't have to be an auto expert to prevent car accidents and expensive repairs. You only have to be mindful.

I don't care what kind of vehicle you drive. It can be a car, van, truck, or SUV. It can cost $1,000 or $100,000. Every automobile shares the same needs. Sure, the specifics vary depending on make and model, but auto repair is easier than you've been led to believe. After you read this book, you might decide to change your own filter.

The auto industry is in my blood. My dad took me to his auto shop for the first time when I was twelve years old. His mechanics got a kick out of seeing a little girl give them a run for their money. Working on cars made me a stronger woman. I don't depend on a man to fix my engine. I can do it myself. I don't freak out when my car breaks down. I investigate the issue and take action right away.

Many women believe fixing cars is a man's problem. Nonsense. Gender stereotypes go both ways. Cooking used to be considered a, "woman's job," so men stayed out of the kitchen. That's no longer true. Times change. Look at it this way. If a handsome man made you a delicious pasta dinner, would you complain? I didn't think so. Don't be afraid to get your hands dirty. Auto repair is empowering.

Why not let a man fix it? Here's a potential problem. What if your car breaks down and no one is there to help you? Getting stranded isn't fun. It's even worse when you don't know how to respond (I'll show you in the next chapter). You need this book, girlfriend. No more auto anxiety. With my help, you will become a safe and confident driver.

Mechanically Yours,

Audra

What to Do When Your Car Breaks Down

Drive every day? Your car could break down sooner or later. You better be prepared. Scared? Don't be. The next time you break down, remember these tips (#3 is simple yet effective).

1. Get off the road.

Don't play chicken!

The sooner you get off the road, the sooner you'll be out of harm's way:

If you're in a neighborhood, try to find a church. If you're in a downtown area, pull over in a business parking lot. If any people are around, ask to use their jumper cables.

If you're on a highway or interstate, pull over on the shoulder. Keep driving until you reach a straight section of the road. Don't stop on a curve where no one can see you.

If your engine comes to a sudden stop, it might be impossible to park in an ideal spot. Simply do your best to get out of harm's away.

2. Call for help.

Got roadside assistance? If so, put that membership to use.

Blocking traffic? If so, call 911 and notify the highway patrol.

Flat tire? Bummer. If you know how, go ahead and put on a spare.

If you're stopped on a busy street, it might be safer to call a tow truck.

3. Chill out.

This is not the time to panic. Close your eyes. Count to ten. Take a few deep breaths. Calm your nerves. Taking a moment to compose yourself will make you feel confident and in control.

4. Let people know you're stuck.

Pop your hood. Turn on your emergency lights. Hang a towel or plastic bag in your window.

Is the sun already down? If so, light a flare so other drivers can see you. No flares? Buy a pair.

Do everything in your power to get the attention of a police officer or somebody who can help you.

5. Expect the best (prepare for the worst).

It's nice to "hope for the best" and "look on the bright-side," but car breakdowns do happen. Be ready.

Buy a first aid and roadside emergency kit. These tools are like a plunger (except more important). Hopefully you'll never need them, but they could prove to be useful in a scary emergency situation.

You Don't Need a Tune Up (Here's Why)

Have you ever got a tune up? Most drivers have.

Cars have changed so much that tune ups are a thing of the past.

This chapter reveals fun and interesting facts about how cars work.

Read closely enough and I bet you will never ask for a tune up again.

How Tune Ups Came to Be

Cars weren't always as high-tech as they are today.

Old cars have parts like carburetors and mechanical fuel pumps.

Do either of those terms ring a bell? If not, don't feel bad. My kids don't know either. These parts aren't even included on modern vehicles.

Vintage cars require more upkeep. They don't come with a fancy computer that monitors their performance. Old cars had mechanical parts that literally made the car spark. Those parts needed to be replaced or adjusted every 6,000-12,000 miles.

Car engines used to be simple. Each spark plug was attached to an ignition wire. For best performance, every wire had to spark the same exact intensity.

Ignition wires made a buzzing noise when they worked well. Mechanics could tell a tune up was done properly when every single wire buzzed in tune. That's where the term, "tune up," came from. Neat, huh?

Why Tune Ups Are No Longer a Thing

Modern cars are completely electronic. They don't even have mechanical parts that can be tuned up. Some auto shops continue to use the phrase, "tune up," because it sounds familiar to customers. Most drivers aren't aware of how much cars have changed.

It's marketing that needs a tune up. Your car is run by sensors and relays. A computer in your engine controls the ignition. Dashboard lights alert you to a need for more specific maintenance. A check engine light identifies potential onset of fuel and emission problems.

Don't ask for a tune up. That might not solve your problem. There isn't a set standard for what tune ups include anymore. It's a different service at every shop. If your auto is having a problem, describe the symptoms as specifically as possible. Your mechanic will offer a solution based on that information.

The Auto Body: How to Take Better Care of Your Car

Cars might seem complicated and confusing in your head.

There are so many engine parts that it's hard to understand how it all works together.

No matter how clueless you might feel, auto repair isn't nearly as difficult as you've been led to believe. I will show you how to treat your car with the care and compassion it deserves.

Preventive maintenance is the tune up of the 21st century.

Have you ever had a doctor or dietitian ask you to make better eating decisions?

It's tempting to call them a "bully" for telling you what to do, but that's not true. Your doctor was trying to save you from potential health problems like diabetes and obesity.

People complain about the high price of fruits and vegetables, while failing to consider long-term consequences. French fries are cheaper than salads, but they can cause weight gain, too. Go overboard and you might to buy medicine or new clothes.

9

This isn't a diet book, so I'll spare you a lecture about the virtues of healthy eating. I'm simply illustrating the reality that preventing a health problem is typically more cost effective than curing one. The same principle can be applied to both the physical body and auto body. I'll demonstrate.

If your hair, nails, skin, bones, and muscles are the "physical body," your car is the "auto body."

The human body requires essential vitamins and minerals to function at its best.

If you don't consume enough of these nutrients, your immune system won't be able to protect you from viruses like the flu.

The auto body is no different. It needs nutrients such as motor oil and coolant to perform at its best. If you don't check those fluid levels at specified times, your engine might die without warning. Not good. Engine replacements can cost $4,000 or more depending on your make and model. Don't risk it.

Both the physical and auto body protect you from harm. A strong immune system protects your physical body from disease and sickness. A well-maintained engine protects your auto body from overheating and other malfunctions. There is a downside: neither body can protect you if you don't take good care of them.

Put yourself first (no, it's not selfish).

Most women discount their own needs.

We're so busy taking care of everybody else that we forget to take care of ourselves.

If you make a habit of neglecting your needs, then your ability to help other people will suffer.

If you don't make time to eat healthy foods, you could end up with a life-threatening disease like diabetes.

If you don't take your car to the auto shop ASAP, you could get stuck with more expensive repairs later.

Make it personal.

See your car as an extension of yourself. Hint: giving it a name might help. Choose a name that makes you smile. Use a friend or relative's name for inspiration.

Treat your car as if it's a long-lost brother, sister, cousin, dog, cat, or person you love. Neglecting your auto's needs is NOT nice. Your vehicle provides you with freedom to travel anywhere on Earth.

Perceived this way, auto repair isn't an inconvenience. It's an investment in your health and longevity. The next time you get upset by a bill at the mechanic, repeat this mantra in your mind. You'll get over it.

7 Simple but Effective Ways to Save Money on Gas

Cars are awesome. How would you go anywhere without a set of wheels? Maintaining a vehicle can get expensive, though.

Cutting your gas bill will help you save money that can be deposited into your car jar. You don't have to cut coupons or price shop. Saving money on gas is easy. Here's how.

1. Carpool.

Work for a big company?

If so, you probably know a coworker who lives in your neck of the woods.

Make new friends and take turns driving so you can split the gas bill in two. Talk about a win/win.

2. Check your air filter.

Some shady mechanics push air filters on drivers who don't really need them (yet).

That doesn't mean air filters are a scam. A clean filter improves air flow in your vehicle.

If an air filter gets clogged, your gas mileage will immediately decrease. So, how often should you change your filter? It depends. Check out the owner's manual for your vehicle (OMV) for more info.

3. Take care of your tires.

Only 15% of drivers know how to check tire pressure. The other 85% are wasting a ton of money.

According to the US Department of Energy, properly inflated tires improve your fuel economy by 3%.

That might not sound like a lot. I'll put it another way. Inflated tires save about seven cents per gallon. How much do you drive? Do the math. I bet the savings will add up.

4. Stop being in such a rush.

Clean air filter? Check. Properly inflated tires? Check. Now take a deep breath and slow down.

Most drivers don't follow the next three tips, because they are in such a big hurry. Friendly suggestion: give yourself at least ten extra minutes to reach your destination.

Driving is stressful when you're worried about being late to work or school or wherever you're going. Don't worry about being too early. Toss a book in your purse. That will occupy you.

Stop slamming the brakes. Be gentle with the gas pedal. Sudden, aggressive motions burn up a whole lot of gas. Why are you in such a rush? Tip: Get in the habit of leaving at least 10 minutes early for work and important stuff.

5. Press the gas pedal gently.

Why would you slam the gas pedal as soon as a traffic light turns green?

For one thing, some drivers might run the red light. Look both ways first to be safe.

In addition, you're not in a road race. Chill out. Flooring the pedal burns an unnecessary amount of gas. Take it easy to instantly improve your fuel economy.

6. Don't tap your brakes excessively.

Avoid sudden, jerky movements. It's better to be gentle. Drive at a steady pace.

If you need to slow down, don't slam the brakes. Simply take your foot off the gas pedal. Your trip will be more fuel efficient. As a bonus, you'll extend the life of your brake pads.

7. Use cruise control whenever possible.

It's hard to sustain a constant speed on a long trip. That's why cruise control exists. Alternating from 65 to 75 MPH burns more gas than maintaining a steady 70 MPH. Use the tools that are available. Your gas bill will thank you later.

5 Common Causes of the Check Engine Light

It's tempting to put off a trip to the auto shop when money is tight. Bad idea. Neglecting a repair today could result in a more expensive repair tomorrow. Take your vehicle to a trusted mechanic soon.

Don't be a victim of auto anxiety. Act now. In the meanwhile, here are five common causes of a check engine light. Being mindful of these issues will make it easier to communicate with auto mechanics.

1. Your oxygen sensor needs to be replaced.

Oxygen sensors analyze the air and fuel in your engine. They pass information to the catalytic converter, which turns dangerous emissions into less harmful substances. In other words, these car parts work together to prevent air pollution.

If your oxygen sensor shuts down, your gas mileage could decrease by up to 40%. It gets even worse. Failing to replace your oxygen sensor could cause the death of your catalytic converter. That would turn a $200 repair into a $2,000 repair. Worth the risk? Nope.

Not sure what's causing your check engine light? Call a trusted mechanic as soon as possible. Do not delay. Putting off an auto repair usually causes more expensive problems to develop. Trust me. I've seen enough broken down cars to know exactly what I am talking about. Don't have a mechanic? No problem. Visit www.WomenAutoKnow.com now. We offer a user generated auto shop directory where female drivers like you share details about their experience. This empowers you with choices for who to trust with your auto's repair and maintenance needs.

2. Your fuel cap is loose.

Don't automatically assume the worst when your check engine light comes on. It only costs a few dollars to replace your fuel cap (and the one you already have might simply need to be tightened).

Leaks, odors, fumes, noises, or jerky motions tend to accompany serious car problems. Nothing like that? It might just be your fuel cap. Pull over, unscrew your cap, and put it back on as tightly as you can.

4. Your spark plugs are failing.

Depending on how long you choose to drive the same automobile, you might never have to replace your spark plugs. In vehicles made after 1996, spark plugs typically last 100,000 miles or more.

If you dream of joining the 200,000 mile club, you'll definitely need to replace your spark plugs eventually. Don't delay. Broken spark plugs can cause permanent damage to your catalytic converter.

4. Your mass airflow sensor is malfunctioning.

Mass airflow sensors (MAF) determine how much air and fuel your engine needs to perform efficiently. If your check engine light displays during a stall, it probably means your MAF needs attention.

5. Your catalytic converter is having problems.

You knew this was coming, right (see #1)? This is the most expensive repair on the list. The good news? As long as you don't put off an oxygen sensor repair, your catalytic converter will be fine.

13 Things Smart Drivers Keep in Their Car

Getting stranded isn't fun, but it's less scary when you keep essential items in your car.

Emergency situations aren't so bad when you're prepared. For the record, I'm 100% aware some of these items might make you think I've been riding the paranoid express.

That's okay. As an auto safety expert, I feel these recommendations are for your best interest. I've fixed enough broken cars to know you'll need most of these items at some point in the future.

1. Pocket Knife

Don't try to scare anyone off with a pocket knife, or they'll pull a Crocodile Dundee on you. There's always someone with a bigger knife! A decent multi-tool pocket knife comes with most prepackaged tool boxes. You can use it to cut things that get caught in your tires (like rope).

2. Battery Jumper Cables

Most people are nice enough to offer help, but they rarely have cables; even though they should, because they've all been stuck in the parking lot of Chuck E. Cheese's at least once in their life, too.

Either get traditional jumper cables or the fancy battery-powered ones. Just hook it up and presto! Wouldn't it feel great to help a fellow driver get back on the road? Saving the day is so much fun!

3. Extra Washer Fluid and a Spare Pair of Windshield Wipers

Washer fluid is a big help when your windows are icy or fogged up. Filling your washer fluid is easier than you think. Ask a mechanic to show you how. Carry a jug of washer fluid in your trunk. Trust me. Wiper blades can break at any time, especially when freezing temperatures arrive. Learn how to change those blades. It's not very difficult. I'm talking less than a minute after you learn how.

4. Flashlight and Extra Batteries

You know you've worried about breaking down in the middle of the night on a dark country road. Spooky! If that ever happens, you'll be relieved to have a flashlight so you can find your way around.

5. First Aid Kit

Cuts and scrapes are a possibility with any auto repair. At bare minimum, keep bandages in your car. You might get to help a friend with a broken nail. There's nothing like helping your fellow woman.

6. Matches or Lighter

Hopefully you'll never be this distressed; but if you ever need

heat in a bad way, matches and lighters do the trick. Having a way to warm up your hands is a blessing when you're stranded on a cold winter day.

7. Ice Scraper and Snowbrush

How many times have you tried to get the snow off your car by hand? Hellooooo frostbite! One time I got desperate enough to use a tree branch I found on the ground. Not effective. I don't recommend it.

8. Paper Towels

Kids are messy creatures, so it's best to be prepared. Keep some paper towels and a small trash-bag in your back seat at all times. You'll be glad to have it the next time they drop an open bottle of apple juice.

9. Duct Tape

What is this, a MacGyver episode? You might think you'll

never really need duct tape. Think again. Someone could clip your car when backing out and knock your mirror off. Tape that baby back on and get moving.

10. Non-Perishable Food and Water

If you get stuck in the snow or spin off the road, your stomach won't know the difference. Getting stranded is already bad enough. It's even worse when you have hangry kids in the backseat. Keep snacks and bottled water in your trunk to be safe.

11. Flares

Ever tried to change a tire in the dark? It's scary with all those cars zooming past you. Flares will get their attention. Incoming drivers will see the bright light in the distance, adjust their speed accordingly, and merge into the other lane to give you space.

12. Shovel, Gloves, and a Blanket

Brace yourself for cold weather. If you ever get stranded without a working heater, you'll wish you had a blanket. Also, there's nothing worse than having to break up ice and snow with your hands. Thinking about it makes me shiver. Use a shovel and gloves to prevent frostbite.

13. Kid Friendly Items

Traveling with children? Toys and games are a must. It's hard to focus on driving when your little angel is throwing a temper tantrum in the backseat. Kids aren't as fussy when they have fun ways to stay busy. If you have a baby, you could even buy an extra pacifier to keep in the car in case they need comfort.

5 Things You Shouldn't Say to a Mechanic You've Never Met

There are wonderful mechanics in the world. You can find a good one at www.WomenAutoKnow.com.

Even so, there's no denying some mechanics view women as easy targets. Protect yourself. Never say these five things to a mechanic unless they've earned your trust.

1. I haven't replaced my tires in years.

It sounds like you're in the market for new tires. Tires can last up to ten years, so let's approach this a different way. Ask the mechanic to inspect your tires and report their conclusions.

2. Do you think I need service?

The mechanic is now thinking… "Goldmine!"

Do yourself a favor and figure out why you're asking for a tune-up.

Did you hear a noise? Do you smell an odor? Has it been a long time since your last auto service? Interested in bonus points? Practice what you'll say before you walk inside.

Here's a good example: "White smoke is coming from my tailpipe. I think it could be an antifreeze issue. The fluid level looks low. Will you make sure?" Now they'll think twice before messing with you.

3. I am thinking about buying this used car. How does it look?

If you have a good relationship with a mechanic, definitely show them the car before you buy it.

You wouldn't purchase a home and then inspect it, would you? No! Treat auto purchases the same way. I'm still including this statement here, because you should be careful about phrasing when you don't know a mechanic.

If you've never been to this auto shop in your life, ask the mechanic to make sure the vehicle is up-to-date with its scheduled maintenance. Do not disclose any more information. Wording the question in this way will protect you from scams and rip-offs.

4. Change my fluids and filters.

Are you certain your fluids need to be changed? They might just need to be topped off.

Ask the mechanic to check – NOT change – your fluids. After they explain their findings, decide whether it's worth the investment. It's money in your pocket.

The same reasoning applies to filters. If your last service was at 35,000 miles – and your filter's recommended replacement is every 30,000 miles – then it should still be in good shape when you check it at 60,000 miles. Do the math and look at your filter. If it doesn't appear to be dirty, it's probably fine.

5. I know it's probably something bad!

How could you possibly know that? You're not a psychic. Take a deep breath to calm down before you go inside. Stick with the facts. Even if an affordable repair is all that's necessary, dishonest mechanics could capitalize on your fear. All they have to do is confirm your negative bias. Don't let that happen.

6 Mistakes Some Mechanics Make

Human error has sunk ships, brought down planes, and ended more than 50% of marriages. Mechanics aren't any more perfect than you. Here are six common mistakes some mechanics make.

1. Wrong Person, Wrong Job

Ask: "When's the last time you saw a problem like this one?"

If the mechanic dodges the question, they might not be qualified (that means go somewhere else).

2. Making goofy mistakes in haste

Never go to an auto shop when you're in a big hurry.

If you've already a month late for an oil change, then it can probably wait one more day.

Rushing a mechanic gives him or her a license to make mistakes. Mechanical errors could cause you to get stranded, so it's best to be patient.

3. Not addressing your real concern

4. Not asking you to authorize a repair

5. Repairing the car without your consent

I'm grouping these problems together, because they can snowball into a nightmare when you don't see them coming.

Expect to be treated like an intelligent human being. Never let a mechanic work on your car before they answer your questions. Otherwise, you might get stuck paying for a service you didn't request.

"Oh, I rotated your tires for you, too."

"Your brake pads needed replacing as well."

"You really needed a new filter, so I tossed one in for you!"

It's completely uncool for a mechanic to do anything to your vehicle without your permission. The repair should be free since they didn't ask. If there's an issue, tell them to put the old parts back and take your business elsewhere.

6. Failing to notify you about a delay.

If you have all the time in the world, this might not be a big deal. If you're in a hurry, check in (especially when your mechanic is waiting on a part to be shipped from another location). If a mechanic does a repair without your authorization, consider it free.

You heard me right. Visualize dinner at a nice restaurant. Your waiter or waitress brings a 20-ounce steak you didn't order. They say it's too late to send it back to the kitchen. Would you pay $50 for a meal you don't want? Nope. Auto repair shouldn't be any different. Don't be bullied. Be empowered. Stand up for yourself.

Working on Cars Made Me a Stronger Woman in 5 Ways

Afraid to get your hands dirty? Don't be! Working on cars is fun and empowering. Being auto aware changed my life in many ways. Here are five big ones.

1. I'm not anxious about auto repairs.

Many women see their auto as a source of stress.

If it doesn't work perfectly every day, they get upset.

Don't put off auto repairs. Take your car to a trusted mechanic at the first sign of a problem. For bonus points, read the owner's manual for your vehicle. It will teach you how to perform basic tasks like checking fluid levels.

2. I don't panic in emergency situations.

Accident prevention comes down to how you react. If you hit a patch of ice, don't freak out. Slamming your brakes will do more harm than good. Take your foot off the gas pedal and keep your gaze forward. Gently accelerate as soon as you regain traction. You've got this.

3. I don't get taken advantage of by mechanics.

Don't ask for a tune-up. Do share details about any strange sights, smells, or sensations you noticed. Being specific will prevent potential confusion and misunderstandings. Want brownie points? Ask to receive a call with a price quote before any work is done.

4. I don't need a man to "save" me if my car craps out.

It's empowering to be able to change my tire without calling a man for help. Sometimes I even get to help a man get his car back on the road. Talk about role reversal. Imagine the stunned look on your husband's or boyfriend's face when you change his tire. Wouldn't that be funny? Yep.

5. I don't take my car for granted anymore (This is huge!).

My car does so much for me. It takes me to work. It takes my kids to school. It takes my family on fun and fulfilling vacations. Since your vehicle adds value to your life in so many ways, it's only fair to return the favor. I bet working on cars will help you become a stronger woman, too. Hey, it doesn't hurt to try.

Drive into Savings, Find a Good Mechanic, Become a Better Driver, and Join the 200K Mile Club with Women Auto Know

Hi. Audra here. Thanks for reading. If you liked this book, I bet you would love my blog (updated every Tuesday morning). Check it out at: www.WomenAutoKnow.com/blog

Feel free to bookmark that page so you don't miss out on tips, tricks, and insights like the ones you saw here. Below is a list of my personal favorites to help you get started.

4 Tire Safety Tips for Teen Drivers – www.WomenAutoKnow.com/tire-safety-tips

5 Signs You're an Aggressive Driver – www.WomenAutoKnow.com/aggressive-driver

6 Signs You Need to Buy a New Car ASAP – www.WomenAutoKnow.com/buy-a-new-car

7 Preventive Auto Repairs You Auto Know – www.WomenAutoKnow.com/preventive-auto-repairs

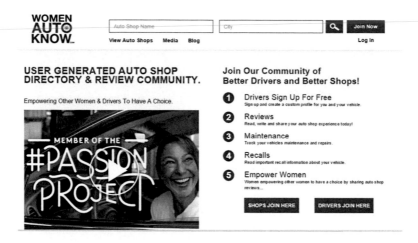

8 Ways to Make a Commute Less Boring – www.WomenAutoKnow.com/boring-commute

9 Ways to Make Long Drives More Bearable – www.WomenAutoKnow.com/long-drives

10 Ways to Find a Good Mechanic Who Will Treat You Right – www.WomenAutoKnow.com/find-a-mechanic

If you want to take good care of your vehicle and become a proud member of the 200,000 mile club, register today at www.WomenAutoKnow.com. Membership is free for drivers and always will be. Feel free to invite your friends, family, and loved ones.

About Audra Fordin

Audra Fordin has been in the auto repair business since she was a little girl working side-by-side with her dad. Great Bear Auto Repair and Auto Body Shop, one of America's leading automotive franchises, felt the crunch of the recession of 2008 just like the rest of the country.

Under Audra's leadership, Great Bear shifted its focus to serving women, families, and the New York community. Growing her business by over 33% in two years, Audra reversed the trend and began sharing her knowledge with other auto shops in the U.S.

Today, thousands of drivers and auto shops are proud members of Women Auto Know, where better drivers find better shops. Drivers take ownership for the condition of their vehicle. Shops promote the philosophy: "Educate Not Intimidate," "Show and Tell," "Tell Not Sell," and "Service Not Sales."

Audra has been featured on Rachael Ray, Anderson Cooper, 20/20, The Today Show, Inside Edition, Good Morning America, and Despierta América. She won NYC's 2011 Small Business of The Year award and is a Girl Scout Outstanding Troop Leader for two years running. She also travels across the country to educate our next generation of drivers with the National Children's Museum.

Visit www.WomenAutoKnow.com to learn more about Audra and Women Auto Know.

Appendix: Preventive Auto Repairs That Will Save Tons of Time, Trouble, and Money

How much? How long? Why does it matter? Do I really need it?

If I had $1 for every time I've heard those questions, I'd be richer than Donald Trump. First: it's important to understand the difference between three different kinds of auto maintenance services:

1. Normal maintenance

2. Extreme maintenance

3. Preventative maintenance

If you don't drive very often and live in a moderate climate where the temperature doesn't swing up or down a lot, normal maintenance is all you need.

If you're a traveling salesman, trucker, cabbie, bus/limousine driver, or somebody else who logs a lot of miles on the road, extreme maintenance might be necessary.

If you want to save money while adding years to your vehicle's life – and possibly join the 200,000 mile club while you're at it – preventative maintenance is your jam.

The following preventive auto repairs are designed to keep your vehicle in tip top condition. Please understand these friendly suggestions do not replace the existing requirements from the manufacturer. Those are mandatory to keep your new vehicle warranty in effect.

Let me be clear. Preventative auto repair services carry a cost. I am not trying to make you go broke. The purpose is to save money in the long-term. Would you rather invest in the health of your vehicle... or risk having to buy a new one sooner than necessary? The first option sounds better to me.

Note: Every auto shop should provide a basic, "once over," inspection at no charge. This is your right. Exercise it. You are giving them an opportunity to earn business from you. They should be happy to give your automobile a glance. It's nice to see a driver being proactive about the condition of their vehicle.

If your vehicle makes a strange sound or swerves to the left or right while you drive, then you should probably ask for a road test, too. How else would a mechanic gather information about the problem? That said, visual inspections are pretty easy. You can do this yourself without any expensive equipment.

Check your wipers. Are they in good shape, or can you tell they have seen better days? If they're in dire straits, get them replaced. It's cheap. While your car is parked in the driveway,

turn on your headlights and blinkers. Do they work? If not, you have a problem. Make an appointment with your mechanic. Don't have one? Visit www.WomenAutoKnow.com. We offer a free user generated auto shop directory.

Open your hood. Don't have a clue what's in front of you? Read your OMV (owner's manual for your vehicle). There will be a diagram that points out the location of your fluids and battery. There are four fluid levels to inspect: oil, coolant, brake fluid, and transmission fluid. If a fluid is low, that means you need to visit an auto shop ASAP. Inspect your battery. Is it completely black? Good. Is there white dust? Uh oh. Sounds like acid corrosion. That means it needs attention.

You're almost done (I promise). Look at your tires. Do you see any holes, tears, cracks, bulges or scrapes? If so, it's time for a replacement. This is urgent. Do not procrastinate. If a tire blows out on the Interstate, you could lose control of your vehicle. 500+ folks die in tire-related traffic accidents per year. 19,000 more get hurt or injured. You do not want to be a part of that statistic.

All of that said, auto repair can be tricky. It's good to be mindful of your vehicle's needs, but you probably shouldn't do any complicated jobs unless you're 100% confident in your ability to do it right. Difficult repairs should always be done by a seasoned pro.

Not sure where to start? Here's a shove in the right direction. Below is a list of suggested preventative maintenance services you should know. I'm also including an estimate of how long each service takes. You'll know you need to organize transportation before, not after you go to the shop. Isn't that convenient?

Transmission Fluid Service

How long it takes: 60 minutes

What it does: Transmission fluid helps your engine operate smoothly. If you run out, expect to breakdown. Please note the timing of this service depends on your climate. The more you drive in extreme conditions, the sooner your transmission fluid needs to be refilled.

Cooling System Fluid Exchange

How long it takes: 60 minutes

What it does: Your car's cooling system is similar to your body's circulatory system. It keeps your engine running at a temperature that isn't too hot or too cold (just right!). Fail to refill your coolant in time and your engine could overheat. Don't risk it.

Air Conditioning Performance Check

How long it takes: 45 minutes

What it does: It's tough to identify the cause of a busted car AC. It could be a leak, faulty part, etc. Please note this service is simply a diagnosis. There could be follow-up jobs depending on the nature of the problem.

Fuel Injection Cleaning Service

How long it takes: 60 minutes

What it does: Your engine's temperature rises when you turn off the ignition. In time, this causes a residue to clog up essential engine parts. If your engine hesitates a lot, consider investing in this service.

Top Engine Cleaning Service

How long it takes: 60 minutes

What it does: This service is similar to the previous one. Residue can build up on other engine parts including your throttle plate and intake runners. If you experience hesitation when accelerating, this could be the cause. Ask a trusted mechanic to verify.

Air Filter Change

How long it takes: 15 minutes

What it does: Everyone has heard a story about a mechanic

selling air filters to drivers who don't need them. It's the oldest trick in the book. This does happen, but that doesn't mean air filters last forever. Air filters power your engine by funneling outside air into your engine. Get it done… just not all the time.

Cabin Air Filter Change

How long it takes: 15-45 minutes depending on make and model

What it does: This is not the same thing as a regular air filter. Cabin air filters prevent certain particles from getting into the air you breathe. I put a time range for this job, because it's harder to reach the cabin air filter on some vehicles than others.

Fuel Filter Replacement

How long it takes: 30 minutes

What it does: Fuel filters trap contaminants in your gasoline. Many new vehicles require the fuel filter to be replaced at the same time as your fuel pump. Check your vehicle's owner's manual for more info.

Brake Service

How long it takes: 45 minutes

What it does: Imagine how scary driving would be without brakes. How would you stop or slow down? No, thanks. Your brake pads consist of friction material, which provide the braking force needed to operate properly. Prevention is key here. Letting your brakes wear down will increase the repair cost.

Brake Fluid Exchange

How long it takes: 30 minutes

What it does: Brake fluids absorb moisture (water) due to the hot and cold cycles required for the fluid to operate correctly. Over time, this can cause the brake fluid to get contaminated, which is why you need to exchange it every now and then.

Power Steering Fluid Exchange

How long it takes: 60 minutes

What it does: Power steering systems have been standard for decades. Power steering fluid needs to be flushed and exchanged at set intervals. Check out your vehicle's owner's manual for specific details.

Timing Belt Replacement

How long it takes: 4 hours

What it does: The purpose of the timing belt is hidden in its name. Timing belts synchronize your engine parts so they fire at the exact right time. If the timing belt breaks, it could cause damage to your engine. Most makes and models suggest replacing the timing belt every 60,000-105.000 miles. Check your timing belt's condition on the lower end of that recommendation to prevent more expensive problems.

Headlight Alignment

How long it takes: 15 minutes

What it does: Have you ever been blinded by the headlights of an approaching vehicle? You probably assumed their brights were turned on, but that's not necessarily the case. Their headlights could have been misaligned. The next time you turn on your headlights, give them a close look. Are both beams of light level with each other? If not, hire a mechanic. Your fellow drivers will appreciate the thought.

Wheel Alignment

How long it takes: 45 minutes

What it does: Misaligned wheels cause tires to wear out faster than they should. Investing in this service pays off quickly due to the high cost of tire replacements. Not sure your wheels are aligned? Pay attention to your vehicle's handling. If it drifts to the left or right, you have a problem.

Manual Transmission Fluid Exchange

How long it takes: 45 minutes

What it does: Manual transmissions are popular, especially in sports cars and high-performance vehicles. These types of vehicles need fluids in addition to the basics like oil and coolant. Read the owner's manual for your vehicle to learn more.

Differential Gear Oil or Fluid Exchange

How long it takes: 45 minutes

What it does: Differential gear fluid lubricates gears and components to transfer power to your wheels. This is true whether you have front-wheel, rear-wheel, or all-wheel drive. This service includes replacing the correct amount and type of fluid, plus any additives recommended by your vehicle manufacturer. Please note there is a similar service called "transfer case fluid exchange" for 4x4 vehicles.

Belts and Hose Replacement Service

How long it takes: 60 minutes

What it does: Your belts and hoses are an important part of your engine and other systems connected to them. Sometimes a belt requiring replacement is easy to see. Hoses may look okay visually from the outside, but most hoses actually fail due an internal breakdown. If one hose fails, it's recommended to replace both since the other could fail soon (and who wants to breakdown in the middle of nowhere?).

Tire Rotation and Balance

How long it takes: 40 minutes

What it does: If your car shakes or shimmies at high speeds, you need a tire rotation. Rotating your tires every 6,000 to 7,500 miles will even out their tread wear. Many mechanics offer a life-time rotation service, which is a wise investment when you trust the shop and don't plan to move anytime soon.

Wiper Blades

How long it takes: 15 minutes

What it does: No one appreciates wiper blades until they get stuck in the rain or snow without them. Don't put yourself in that situation. Be mindful of their condition. If they have seen better days and inclement weather is coming soon, get them replaced to be safe.

Battery Replacement

How long it takes: 30 minutes

What it does: The battery is your car's heart. Your engine couldn't start without it. Remember your battery's birthday. Replace it on time to save yourself from having to call a tow truck or ask for a jump.

Recommended Service Intervals

"An ounce of prevention is worth a pound of cure." It's cheaper to prevent car problems than it is to repair them. This is why your owner's manual suggests getting your vehicle serviced at specific times. The details vary depending on make and model, but the list below is fairly typical.

15,000 Miles

If you own a used car, this might not apply to you; in that case, skip to the number of miles that most accurately reflects your odometer. Your auto will require an oil + filter change, tire rotation, and safety inspection at this time. Note: those three things should occur during every service following this one, but I'm only going to mention them here. For brownie points, ask the mechanic to check for recall information. Brake pads could require replacement at this time depending on your make and model.

30,000 Miles

At this point, some of your automobile's fluids might need attention: coolant, brake fluid, and transmission fluid in particular. Ask the mechanic to check the appearance of your air and fuel filter. Depending on context, your tires and/or brake pads could require replacement. Note: this is true for every service beyond this one. Brakes and tires are highly important. Always be aware of their condition.

45,000 Miles

Your car has put in tons of work at this point, so it's time to check the condition of your brakes, belts, and hoses. Watch out for leaks or noises that could signal a problem. You might need to replace your engine air filter and/or cabin air filter (not the same thing) depending on the mechanic's findings.

60,000 Miles

If you have a car that's more than ten years old, this service could be expensive. If you have a newer car, this service won't be so bad. What's the difference? Spark plugs and timing belts have longer lifespans on new cars than old cars. It all comes down to your situation. Check your OMV for more information.

75,000 Miles

This service is no different than a basic service (oil change, tire rotation, and safety inspection), but you might have to replace your shock absorber depending on its condition. Ask the mechanic to check it out.

90,000 Miles

If you have a car that's more than ten years old, this service shouldn't be so bad, provided you made the proper investments at 60,000 miles. If you have a newer car, this could be your most expensive service yet. Filters, coolant, transmission fluid, differential fluid, spark plugs, and timing belts could all require replacement at this time. I know that sounds expensive, but remember: preventing a problem is always more expensive than repairing one. Choose wisely. Start saving ahead of time so you'll be ready.

100,000 Miles

Did your car make it to the 100K club? Wow. Congrats! Now let's try to double it. All of the issues I mentioned at the 90,000 mark could be relevant here. Climate, road conditions, amount of driving, and other issues will determine the exact timing of your repair and maintenance needs. Regardless, expect your vehicle to require attention soon, because you can't drive 100,000 miles without wear and tear.

105,000 Miles

This service is all about the timing belt. If you haven't replaced it yet, now is the time. Trust me. It costs $500-900 to replace a timing belt for the purpose of prevention. If your timing belt breaks, it could cause $2,000 or more in damage to your engine. Waiting is too risky. Act now. Depending on your context, your engine mount and coolant hose could require replacement at this time.

120,000 Miles

The details of this service are similar to the 60,000 mile service. If you have an older vehicle, expect to get hit with a big bill, because it's time to change those fluids again. If you have a newer vehicle, you might luck out with an oil change and tire rotation (cross your fingers!). For brownie points, ask the mechanic to check the condition of your vehicle's suspension system.

135,000 Miles

This service is a repeat of what occurred at 75,000 miles, except there are more potential problems due to the age of your vehicle.

150,000 Miles

Expect this service to be a doozy. Coolant, brake fluid, transmission fluid, spark plugs, air filters, and fuel filters could all require replacement. Beyond this service, your auto's needs will depend more on your individual situation – climate, road conditions, and driving habits – than anything else.

If you want to join the 200,000 mile club, pay attention to what your automobile expresses through sights, sounds, smells, and sensations. Write down exactly what happened and get that information to a mechanic as soon as possible.

Conclusion

This is not meant to be an exhaustive list of every auto repair you will ever need. It's simply a list of highly important preventive services that every responsible driver should understand.

Important: Follow the manufacturer's recommendations first and foremost. Afterwards, reference this list to find out what the repair involves and how long it will take. If necessary, organize transportation before going to the shop.

Thanks for reading. I know you're busy, but may I ask for a tiny favor? I want to educate and empower female drivers like you. Leaving a short-and-sweet review on Amazon would help me do so. Got a sec? Tell me what you thought about the book at this link: www.WomenAutoKnow.com/review